Faith in Flames

Faith in Flames

Jane Grayshon

Illustrated by Stephen Darlington

When you walk through the fire,
* you will not be burned;*
* the flames will not set you ablaze.*
                                    Isaiah 43:2

Hodder & Stoughton
LONDON SYDNEY AUCKLAND TORONTO

Scripture quotations are taken from the New International Version of the Holy Bible, unless otherwise indicated.

British Library Cataloguing in Publication Data

Grayshon, Jane
  Faith in flames.
  1. Christian life – Devotional works
  I. Title
  242

  ISBN 0-340-51740-9

Published by Hodder and Stoughton,
a division of Hodder and Stoughton Ltd,
Mill Road, Dunton Green, Sevenoaks, Kent TN13 2YA
Editorial Office: 47 Bedford Square, London WC1B 3DP

Photoset by Rowland Phototypesetting Ltd
Bury St Edmunds, Suffolk

Printed in Great Britain by Clays Ltd, St Ives plc

Contents

Part I

FLASHES
Images in the fire

The flash of (love) is a flash of fire;
a flame of God himself.
                                Song of Songs 8:6 JB

When I was a child each bedroom in our home had a real, coal fireplace. The fires were seldom lit: that was a treat reserved only for when we were ill.

And what a treat that was for us! Suddenly the darkness of illness was shed, in every sense. The bedroom became alive.

"Watch the patterns dancing on the ceiling, my darling," my mother would say as she bent over me to kiss me good-night.

For hours I would lie watching the flashes of brightness as the iron fireplace gave out its warm glow. Sometimes, in a momentary flash, there would be a picture either in the flames themselves or, more often, in the orange shadows above my bed. It mattered no longer that I could not sleep.

That house has been sold now. No longer do we even have a hearth for a real fire. But I can close my eyes and be transported straight back to the blip-blipping of the flames licking round the coal. Once again there are momentary pictures in my mind's eye.

This section contains some of the pictures. As the Song of Songs describes, there can be flashes in which we see a flame of God Himself reflected in the fire of life.

1

As inevitably
as a stream flows
towards the sea

so am I
drawn towards You

Not to be lost
a tiny stream
in a vast ocean

Our place of meeting
is but a beginning
of the immeasurable

2

There's a score across the sky, there
Where an aeroplane's just been
Cutting it and marring it
Slicing it in two

There's a score across my abdomen
Where surgeons' knives have been
Cutting me and marring me
Slicing me in two

There's a score across my life, Lord
Where deepest hurts have been
I am so marred
and cut apart
in many, many ways

> The trail above me's fading now
> Blown across the sky
> The scar across my abdomen
> is fading with the years
> But the scar across my life, Lord,
> Never can be swept away

Save me from seeing only hurt:
Show me Your hand as well.
For with one touch
You leave Your mark
Changing me, not marring me,
Leading me
to You.

3

With hypnotic rhythm
The seaweed sways
around the rock from which it grows;
Brown shiny smoothness
undulating,
Broken suddenly
by a wave rushing in.

Flooded by new salty depth
its fingers unfurl
Floating upwards, not fighting,
Swept round in a great arc from its roots.
Then,
unthreatened even by counter-currents
it gracefully turns
Swinging with circular motion
Sucked under and backwards
to surge once more with successive swells.

> And I am amazed;
> Though the tide is so strong
> All movement is gentle;
> With graceful motion
> it curls
> in unison with the sea

Lord, You are my rock:
Be to me the element
in Whom I am at ease;
Rooted in You
Let me grow outwards
Unafraid of threatening waves which flood me

Unfurl my frozen fingers
stiff with holding to the rock,
Till I'm floating with new freedom
Buoyed up by the throb of Your love

Like a dancer with her partner
Sweep me up in Your strong hold;
And Lord, give me the grace
To sway in step with You.

The spider, falling
gently unravels
his gossamer thread

abandoning himself to his drop

delicately weaving
a pattern
where he's been held

> When I start to sink
> into a deep abyss
> I plummet, panicking
> Hands tight with terror
> clinging to You

Watching the spider
I relax as I realize
I can trust Your tenacity

> For nothing, and no-one
> can snatch me from
> Your
> secure hold

> So I'll abandon
> my whole weight
> to You

And when I doubt
I'll look to this web
a testimony to the spider's falls
and to his safety

And I'll trust again
For I'll know
that wherever I've fallen
You've woven a thread
a shining testimony
to Your design
wrought from my falls

Your goodness sometimes seems
     over there
        out of reach

          I see glorious displays
             of promises fulfilled
                in others

                And I am blind
                   to the signs of Your goodness
                      in me

                   But a rainbow's end is never visible
                   to those who stand below;
                      It's only seen to reach
                         elsewhere —
                            never overhead

                      In the midst of turmoils
                         eyes smart
                            with sharp stings of rain
                            and sight is dazzled
                            by bright beams of sun:
                               So what's visible
                               is hidden
                               by transparent sensations

                      Lord God, my Father:
                      May the knowledge of Your
                            promise
                      glow more richly than my
                            doubts;
                      For You accept
                      what I count as waste
                      bestowing Your radiance
                      until I become
                      a crucible for Your beauty

How I long to be bubbly again
like the Lucozade on my locker!

Yet
Only when it is poured out
into its glass
does it sparkle and dance with fizz

Only
when I am poured out
into Your hands
do I sparkle and dance with fizz

My God
Infuse me with the bubbles
of Your life in me!

It's dark.
It needs to be so, for
my strained eyes could not endure a stark lamp glaring out.
And so – how thoughtfully! – Matthew's opened my
   curtains
inviting the orange glow from the streetlamp,
      restfully subdued,
to glimmer quietly into my room.

It takes time to take in –
   lying passively
   eyes fixed but not focused
   lids lifting with momentary gaze –
a pattern's reflected over there, on my wall.

That panel of orange light
is chequered
with tiny squares of shadow
cast by the net curtain
filtering the dim light
     like grilled bars
     like a cage
     like a prison.

Then with sudden roar
a car races by
headlights darting round the circuit of my walls
before, in a flash, it has gone.

    In my moments of knowing deeply
    the light of Your presence,
      do not pass me by
        in a flash which brings fear
      nor dazzle me
        with full beam which blinds.

And when I'm left
with the quiet constancy
of the patterns of Your light
shining (even while I'm imprisoned),
    may I not kick uselessly at the bars
    which are but shadows of imperfection.

One day I'll not be confined to this cage of life
I'll be on the other side of the net
with no filters between You and me,
no shadows to cast:
only Your light

        But now
        flood Your light
        through the filters of my imperfection
        freeing me to gaze on You.

Like a mist upon the sea
Sleep lies
Elusive
Beyond reach
    from the island in which I am stranded
    from this body in which my soul camps

I want to chase that mist
To row out towards it
  But it moves ahead of me
  Like a promise-filled rainbow
    ungraspable
    unattainable

I want to capture it in a glass jar
As on childhood collecting outings
And, screwing down its lid,
Keep it till I want it.

"I'm ready now!" I would cry
And, eagerly opening its lid
Hoping . . .
  But it would have changed
  Precipitated
  into tiny droplets of water
  dancing their patterns in the jar
Disappointing . . .

I have to wait
For sleep to creep up to my island
First lapping dreamily on the shoreline
Then nearer
Until, sweet joy!
It covers me completely

    . . . Like Your grace, Lord.

When I think I can earn it
It slips further from me
Like that rainbow of promise

Only without chase
    without pursuit
    without my pathetic attempts to earn it
Can I be overtaken
        embraced
        enfolded
By Your sweet grace!

Not mine to demand
nor snatch aggressively
But to receive
In Your time . . .
                My God.

9

I hear the voice of sleep
   calling
Like a ghost
   beckoning.
I answer, turn and search
   groping.
But she has vanished
     intangible
     silent.
Her shadow haunts me still;
Yet she will not revisit me.
Elusive phantom!
Oh that you would overtake me now!

Wind-blown, leaf-swept
bare trees.
But see!
Not all are bare:
Not that tree.
Twelve leaves are still there . . .

Branches holding
Fingers stretching
As with desperate resolve
To cling on . . .

Cling on to what has been:
Cling on to new Spring birth-that-was
Cling on to lush Summer growth-that-was
Cling on to rich Autumn beauty-that-was
Last dregs now . . .

Just
a tree.
Always there
hiding beneath
Now seen:
Now
Just a tree
with twelve leaves

Lord,
Give me new birth
But not to cling on to;
May I always be renewed

Give me lush growth
But not to cling on to;
May I always be growing

Give me rich beauty
But not to cling on to;
May I always be Yours

Let me cling only
to being
bare before You.

Part II

FLAMES
Sparks of faith ignited

He showed you his great fire,
and you heard his words from out of the fire.
                              Deuteronomy 4:36

This group of poems has been sparked off by fresh inspiration in God. Each poem emerged from a moment of knowing deeply the flame of His presence burning within my heart.

Flames appear to be only destructive. However, they have frequently been a sign of God's presence.

In the Bible flames were the place where God spoke His promises to Moses (Exodus 3). They were a sign of God's guidance to the children of Israel, every night of their journey to the promised land (Exodus 13). Flames were a sign of God's closeness for Manoah and his wife (Judges 13). They gave proof of God's power to Elijah and King Ahab competing on Mount Carmel (1 Kings 18). Flames were the place where God protected Shadrach, Meshach and Abednego from the fiery furnace (Daniel 3). At Pentecost, flames were a sign of God's special anointing by the Holy Spirit (Acts 2).

For myself, too, flames which have threatened to be harmful have actually become the place where God has shown Himself to be very specially close. The poems in this section reflect this sense of God's touch, when my faith has ignited and is burning strongly within.

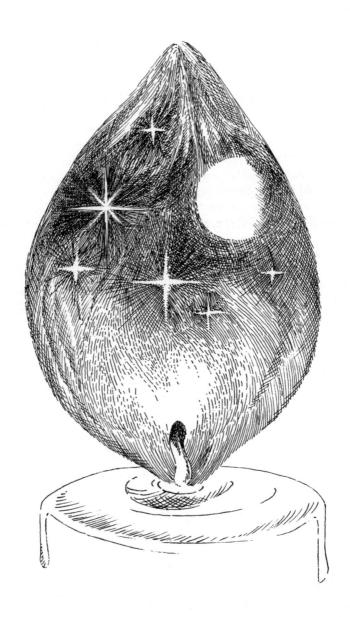

My eyes like to see
the lovely stars in the sky
shining
like diamonds and crystals

and the sun above my head
and the moon
shining and shining

Eyes are shiny, too,
and the golden water shines

My eyes like to see candles
and the light in the sky

God will give me a new heart
that shines with happiness inside me

                    Angus aged 6

12

Hungrily
I seek You
to learn of You
to feed from You
greedily

And as I read
and as I write
    I am drawn close
    by Your arms
    held
    as a babe

Who, having suckled,
drops into sweet slumber:
filled, for that hour,
in deep contentment
with naked embrace of intimacy

    Lord, may my seeking
    not only be frenzied activity;
    teach me contentment
    until I am not ashamed
    to find myself slumbering
    in Your hold

Let me dare
to stop swimming

to turn on my back

not
in order to drown
uselessly

but
to discover
floating

Let me dare
to stop trying
to do Your will

Let
Your will be done
in me

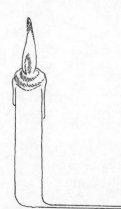

14

At times when it's calm
I'm aware of Your depths
and I float on Your love
and I move with the swell

But at others, it seems
I'm stuck at the edge
being crushed on the rocks
by the waves crashing in

And I've tasted the salt
where the waves break ashore
casting spray which tastes bitter
and drenches my hair

Take my hand, let us run
let us leap out beyond
Till we're out in the depths
and together, we'll swim

When Your water surrounds me
then we are as one

I pray for Your strength
And You give me weakness
Telling me that that is how
Your strength is made perfect

I pray for Your riches
And You give me poverty
Telling me that that is how
Your kingdom is found

I pray for Your life
And You bring me to the brink
Telling me that Your Resurrection
Was born out of death

I pray for forgiveness
And You give me great joy
Telling me
That You delight in me
And You treasure me as a jewel

My Lord and my God
Your ways are not my ways
I can but reply
With thanks from my heart.

Too often
I treat You
as a coffee-break God

Giving You a slot
in my day
from which I leave
refreshed
but ready to return
to "the rest of life"

> You are
> a living fountain
> welling up constantly
> bubbling perpetually
> never to be confined
> to one cup
> to be drunk, like a dose,
> and then emptied.
> Once each day
> (or twice, or three times!)
> ticked off, and signed.
> Drug administered

No, Lord;
may I drink from You always!
For the more I sup
then the more I thirst
for "the rest of my life"
to be irrigated
by channels which overflow
from a constant exchange
at Your wellspring.

"Switch off the television!
There are too many children past crying
       too many parents past caring
       too many governments past sacrificing:
I loathe to see
to be shown undeniably
that my help is merely
  a drop in the ocean."

Yet
       One drop of dye
       changes
       all of the mixture

       One candle's flame
       lights
       all round this dark room

       One pinch of salt
       flavours
       all of my casserole

          Creator God
          give us the courage
          to change our world's hue;
          Let more of Your Light
          spread out from ourselves
          giving back to this planet
          the flavour of You.

"Sorry your wife has walked out.
We're thinking of you."
   (Please, if you care,
   Just bring round a pie
   And leave it on my doorstep . . .)

"Sorry your man is in prison.
We'll pray for him."
   (Please –
   Perhaps he can pray
   For you too . . .)

"Sorry you're shy: you needn't be.
Just call round on us
Some time."

"Sorry you're ill
   your baby's deformed
   you've no-one to marry
   you can't have a child
Can't talk now – my family's waiting.
Another time . . ."
   (Please,
   Say nothing
   If you don't really care . . .)

"Sorry you've problems
Do come and talk
We'll help on our terms
On our ground
Any time . . ."

I'm sorry our compassion
is held at arm's length:
we shrink from involvement
lest we, too, be hurt.

Give me courage, Lord Jesus,
to pray for Your care:
You offer the privilege
of hurting through You.

You hear the cries of many
You give them My love;
Bring Me your own tears dear one
Listen to Me weep, with you.

You hold the hand of many
Your touch brings them My care;
Rest your weary arms awhile
Feel My arms round you.

You see the pain of many
You bear so much with them;
Rest your tired eyes, dear one
Feast them solely on Me.

You bear the cares of many
You hold them in My name;
Rest your heavy heart in Me
In your heart, I AM.

Blue flowers
first seen
boasting their beauty

then plucked
to be treasured
in a vase

Admiration became
their end
Oh, vanity!

For they closed, to become
green stems only
blue flowers hiding

Father, forgive
our vanity

our beauty within us
is not to be admired
nor be plucked out of context
to be preserved

but simply to be
a spontaneous delight
to You

Next day
unwatched
in windowsill vase

blue flowers
first peeped
then ventured out

unselfconsciously
in sun's steady rays
opening fully

Christ, Your rays
flood steadily
edging into closed emptiness

seeking potential
reviving weary wilting

opening myself
unselfconsciously
to bask in Your Spirit

until, once more,
I can respond
with fresh rapport
and unfaltering gaze

Part III

FURNACE
Refinement in the heat

These (trials) have come so that your faith – of greater worth than gold, which perishes even though refined by fire – may be proved genuine and may result in praise, glory and honour when Jesus Christ is revealed.

1 Peter 1:7

God has been described as being "like a refiner's fire" (Malachi 3:2). And there have been moments in my life when I have sensed a little of God's refining furnace. The poems in this section were written in such times.

I once read that a refiner used to sit in front of his fire with the molten metal ore in a crucible. To test the purity of the metal, he would peer into the crucible and see the reflection of his own face. Only when all the impurities had been purged was his refining complete. The reflection would be perfect.

I was thrilled. In God's hands my white-hot pain need not be the destructive force it seems. It can be the furnace in which God, like a refiner, is allowing the impurities of my life to be removed. And afterwards He will look to see His face reflected in me, just as He looks to each one of us to reflect His glory. That is the very purpose for which He created us.

It is reminiscent of diamonds. Diamonds are formed under intense heat and pressure. And God promises, "You will be . . . a royal diadem in the hand of your God" (Isaiah 62:3).

Yet the refining process feels far removed from anything valuable such as pure gold or diamonds. In the midst of a furnace, it feels like hell itself.

I have prayed to be filled with God's warmth; I have even sung the hymn asking God's Holy Spirit to "Melt me . . .". But as I confessed in an earlier book, *A Pathway Through Pain*, as soon as I have come close to the heat of my furnace, I have wanted to shrink from it. I have imagined that it would be better for me if God gave me the gentle warmth of compassion than the white-hot heat of pain.

And yet, His furnace has not consumed me. My spirit has been inflamed, but not incinerated. And perhaps I am a little nearer to saying, along with St Paul, "We, who with unveiled faces all reflect the Lord's glory, are being transformed into his likeness with ever-increasing glory" (2 Corinthians 3:18).

Whenever I hold trustingly to that hope, then I can thank Him for His furnace.

It's like an Arctic hibernation
Pain

When summer's fun
stops
waiting to resume
after winter's finished
and sun will rise again

Like a sentence
in an igloo

Where reality is
distant
Except, of course, for pain
which blocks out all else
like a thick drift of snow

> Have the nights to grow yet longer
> ere the thaw will come . . . ?

Others' words are
muffled
absorbed by the snow
My cries sound all the louder
entrenched within this hole

Winter is worsening
Outside hope is not yet

Into this hibernation, come, Lord:
  Be my flame
  my warmth
  my light
  my hope!

22

They say
we need joy
to bear pain

You've shown
we need pain
to know joy

. . . Your joy

23

The corridor of my life
unfolds steadily ahead

And I venture
from one pool of light
to the next
each time I take a pace

    Tantalized by hope
    disappointed by sameness

And so I learn
the importance of this moment

And I sit awhile
on rough stone ledge
    (who has sat here before me
    in need of a break from their walk?)
basking in the sun's rays
looking out
to where birds sing in freedom
to where the sun shines strongly
warming my back

Until I am ready
to face once more
the shadows

    It's the pillars which cast the shadows
    undergirding, supporting pillars
    Essential to strength

Pain's constrictions
   contradict smugness
   confining
   coercing

Like a drawstring
   gathering in the fullness of my life
   restricting
   restraining
   tightening limitations around me.

Unable to escape
I am able only to accept

And I am loosed

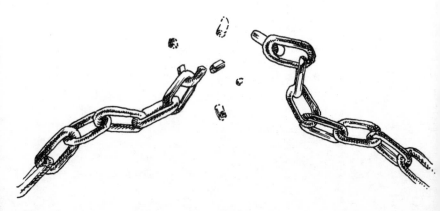

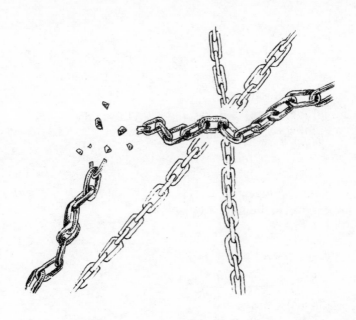

For when I am broken
So too are those boundaries
Which make me look whole

Free to be fragmented
I am drawn to my Father
Whose one caress
Gathers me gently
With whispered promise
To make me whole
His way.

It is the easy way

> to dwell on what we'd like to do
>> but cannot

> to mourn what might have been
>> but is not

> to weep for what was nearly done
>> but not quite

That way is wide
but is not Your way:

> You fulfil
>> Your own desires

> You nurture
>> what You love

> You treasure
>> those You create

Be Lord of my life, Sovereign God!

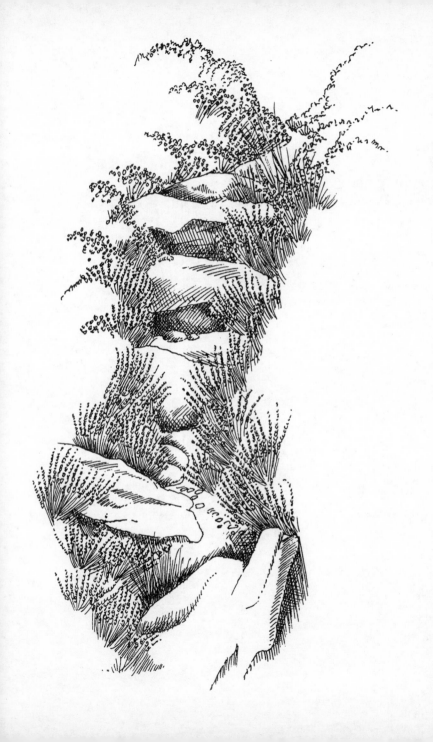

26

Screens drawn securely round my iron bed
Sever pain from those outside it
   They do not need to look at agony

Parting protective partitions, people
Barge bravely between broken barriers
Until, tiptoeing towards me
They enter my ebbing energy existence

     They've stepped over the boundary
     Into my life –
     May I step into theirs?

Tonight,
while pain increases
and nausea, too,
it's like
a huge wave
rising higher than others
   till it towers above me

And I am afraid
because I know
it could crash down
on me
(it has before)

and my head will reel
with the pounding of foaming froth
and the weight of the water . . .

It may overcome me one day!

But I'll ask my God
   to help me to ride
   across this wave
   which curls around with menace

And I'll picture those surfers
   who are not afraid
   but who ride big waves:
   reining the power of the water
   to propel them
   to new places

And I'll take God's hand
   and, balancing,
I'll be held in His power
   which is perfected in weakness

So I'll be led to new places
   His goals
where God will have done new work

And I can rest again
in the eddies of His shelter

Do not kiss me now
Do not come too close
It's every breath which I must breathe
Now
and again now . . .

> I hear a groan with each one
> Is that my voice?
> I do not mean to grunt.
> If I hold my breath
> Does that help?
> . . . I cannot.
> My body's past such pride.
> Instead I'll delay each one . . .

Just stroke me now
My arm,
My forehead,
Run your fingers through my hair.
Without words,
Soothe me
Reach me
in this world with no words
this world where tears will not flow
for anguish.

> Ah! Staccato stabbing
> Pain piercing
> Throbbing
> Punctuated by these cries
> Suppressed
> But not silenced.

> Would that this were singing
> and not a cry of distress!
> Oh my God; my God! . . .

Accept each groan
each involuntary groan
and make it into
a song for You.

My life is on fire

and I am trapped
as by choking fumes
in a tunnel
from which I cannot escape

Pain burns, like a furnace,
until life's very substance
seems to turn to ash

And my faith is in flames:

      Is it not folly
      to trust still in a loving God?

      Is it not folly
      to know disappointment
      yet still, to hope on?

. . . Yet, years on
these flames have never consumed

You have ignited
the dying embers of my soul
fanning them
into inextinguishable hope

You've shown me
the mystery
of Your miraculous

      For this place of flames
      is holy ground

      And I can but bend
      to remove my shoes
      and worship You

            . . . Holy God

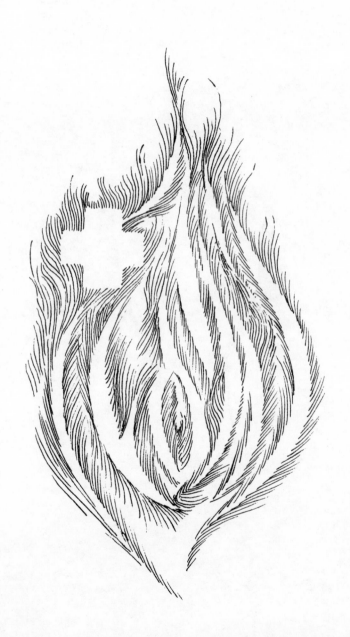

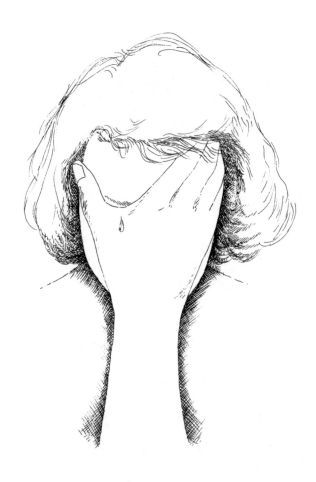

Do not weep
when my body will rest at last

Do not weep
when its loud demands
are silenced at last

Do not weep
when writhing has ceased
and I can lie quietly
beside still waters

Or if you do:
    if tears well up
    in the chalice of your soul
give Him your tears

And let Him change them
into rich wine
consecrated to Him

I've been dreaming
of a painless place

Help me not to live for dreams
Extinguish my greed
which makes me want
more than I need

Give me a vision of Yourself
and do not delay!
lest I drown in myself

Part IV

FLICKERS
Hope from dying embers

He will not put out a flickering lamp . . .
Isaiah 42:3 GNB

One winter's evening at about ten o'clock the surgical ward was hushed for the evening. A friend, Graham, had slipped into the hospital to visit me after I had undergone yet another operation.

As he prepared to leave Graham chose a few verses from the Bible to encourage my flagging spirits.

"We rejoice in our sufferings," he read quietly, "because we know that suffering produces perseverance; perseverance, character; and character, hope. And hope does not disappoint us . . ." (Romans 5:3–5).

Poor Graham! He had only reached thus far when suddenly I burst out indignantly, in front of the ward full of patients, "But hope *has* disappointed me! And God has disappointed me! I've prayed, and hoped, and still I am left in pain. Well there's no hope left now . . ."

It seemed my faith had turned to ashes. Hope seemed dead.

Yet, feebly, falteringly, there was a flicker which remained. If I leaned my hope, not in what God could do for me, but rather on who God is to me, then there was a tiny glow among the otherwise dying embers.

This group of poems hints at the shafts of God's light in the midst of my despair. It tells of the flickers of hope in Him when other hopes are disappointed. It is about flickers which revive when faith is rekindled.

If I lift my eyes
I wish only to be
high on those hills
   exhilarated
   by breathtaking views
   and by the achievement of arriving.

Open my eyes to where I am, Lord.
Your carpet of exuberant richness
is not only above me,
unreachable,
but also beneath my feet
even when I walk in deep valleys.

Limp curtain
dangles heavily
beside an open window

Like my limp body
dangling heavily
beside an open window
between life and Life

But there is no despair
in cool breath of wind
the curtain swings lightly
        rippling freshly
        unfurling freely
        bringing hope . . .

    Hope because there is movement
    Hope because there is freshness
    Hope because there is new life
    opening the curtain barrier with new vigour

Wind of the Spirit,
    blow on me too!
cause me to ripple with Your freshness;
unfurl me into a new freedom:
    the freedom of my life in Yours
    on either side of the open window.

When I cling to what I want
    I am heading only towards death
When I dwell on what hurts me
    I allow myself to be more hurt
When I harbour grudges against those who do not
        understand me
    I close a door to forgiveness
When I shrink back from giving
     a silent gesture of love
     a quiet word of reassurance
    I am strangling kindness and compassion
     stifling their growth
     choking their breath

But You who are Life,
The One who revives,
    You do not leave me choking

You come to me
    offering the moment
    when more of myself
    can be made alive
    in You

You come to me
    offering the moment
    when more of Yourself
    can be made alive
    in me.

Yesteryear's streams
Of living water
Now have ceased
With stagnating stench

Yet You redeem!
The oasis grave
Is marked not with wreaths
But pink bushes
Bursting their beauty
Breathing new birth

Your every touch
Transfigures into glory
Heralding hope
Cultivating courage

> So I dare to return
> Even
> To my old oases
> Of silted-up spirituality

And see!
Shame can be shed;
In the wake of Your presence
Rise rose-coloured rushes
Once again
You have redeemed

> Tentatively
> Tremblingly
> I trust Your touch
> And I sense a trickle
> Of Your Living Water
> Flowing once again.

36

At rock bottom
I feel worthless
Overshadowed
By the heights others reach

But You never look down on me
You are within me
Your light shines out from me
Casting rays for others to see
Rekindling hope
Repeatedly

> With You
> I am a light
> Even
> When I am low.

My heaviness reminds me
that I am like clay
wearied, this night,
by the weight of water

Yet, without water
clay is but useless dust
unable to be moulded

Without You
I am useless dust

Give me, I pray,
a vision of Yourself
as my potter

Deliver me from dread
of drudgery and duty
let me rest my heaviness
on Your wheel

And pour Your water of life
to make me more malleable

Let me feel Your hands
moulding
that I may welcome
every turn of transformation

When those things I cannot do
or dare not do
are misunderstood

And I am told I lack faith
or am called cowardly
or lazy
(if only by myself!)

Then I need Your comfort, Lord.

Only in the security
of being within You
do I dare open myself
to being misunderstood

Do I dare ask for Your kind of care?
  when it asks me to reach out to hearts which are hurt,
  to walk through deep valleys where tears flow from pain,
  to cry out with mercy to those who do wrong,
            to shout for injustice,
            yet love those who hate . . .

  Your care is such
  that You willingly give:
  You seek to show love
  not be loved in return.

When I've something precious
that's snatched right away,
more quickly I turn
to the wrong and my hurt;

  But then, even then,
  Your compassion won't fail:
  still, You give generously
  and graciously, and well.

I can't do all that!
But I'll pray for the seeds
and I'll ask them to grow;
  but slowly, my Father
  or You'll leave me behind.

Caught off guard, I find
My dreams colouring
My imagination flowing
And I want to enjoy it.

Reason is an intrusion to my fantasy
I want to push it away; to bargain with it
And say, "But this is only in my thoughts.
Giving rein to them will do no harm . . ."

When I do not want You to quell what entices me
Nor to label as impurity what I want to enjoy;
　　I need You, my Father.

When darkness masquerades as light
Presenting itself as something harmless
　　I need You, Holy Spirit.

Let me hear Your voice, Lord.
Not such discipline as makes me run away
For I do not come up to Your standards.
But when I do not want Your prompting, Your purity;
When I push You away, and bargain with You
　　Let me hear You then. Especially then.

Catch me off guard, my God.
Colour my dreams with Your glory.
Draw my imagination to flow towards You
And renew my desire to enjoy You.

Part V

FLARES
Beacons on the hill

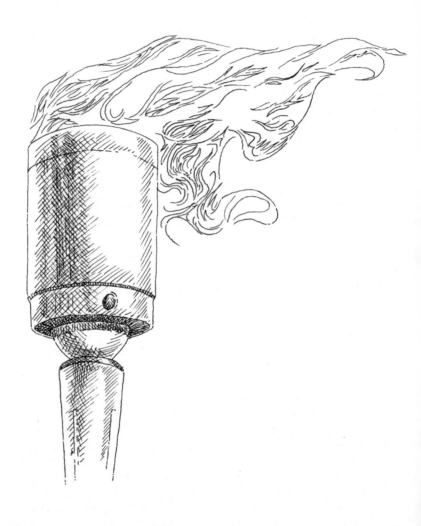

You shine
like stars in the universe . . .
Philippians 2:15

High on a dark hillside north of Athens, before dawn one Easter Sunday morning, tiny dots of torchlight moved silently between the trees. No figures were visible; only the flares which each carried to light his way towards the village church.

The scene is as memorable as any parable. We are like lights on a dark hill. We carry the Light of the world within us. We shine like stars in the universe: not because we are good, but because Christ shines through us.

When I look to others whose lives shine in this way I am often moved and inspired. To know them is like coming to know God Himself. They are like the star which guided the wise men, because they point me towards the place where Jesus is to be found.

But they are the exception. More often our lives point to God's character by way of contrast. I see attitudes in myself which make me think, "Lord God, we are such a poor reflection of You."

I was dismayed, at first, to find that this section contains more about bad examples than good ones. But these poems are not intended to be romantic or glossy. They are conversations with God about the reality of my experience. And even hurts have not always been negative. When other people have hurt me, they have also forced me to rely less on them, and more on God. In nudging me thus towards God they have actually helped me to reach a deeper understanding of God Himself.

And I am consoled, too, to draw a parallel with the light and darkness in outer space. There, the light is dazzling bright – and yet it is seen as blackness in which only the planets reflect the sun's rays. Earth is like a sparkling Christmas jewel – except, that is, its night-time side. Then it is a silhouette, outlined by the brightness of stars behind. It is in this way that other people's dark side can actually highlight God's brightness.

That nurse over there
   the one who is pouring a drink
   for the lady in the end bed
   whose thirst is never quenched –
She is the kind of person
Who gives the extra touches;
Nothing is too much for her.

   She chatters when she's bathing me
   Telling me of life outside these dreary walls.
   She listens when I talk to her
   Sensing when I need to laugh, to weep, to complain.

And when I'm sick
She lays her hand upon my brow
   with caring touch
   and soothing words
   and a cooling sponge
She wipes away gently the sweat of my exhaustion.

And when I've done
She lays me back upon soft pillows
Brushing my hair across fresh sweet-smelling whiteness
   away from my face
   away from my fears within.

And You, my God,
My Comforter –
You are the kind of person
Who gives the extra touches;
Nothing is too much for You
No price too high.

   You poured out Yourself
   until You, too, knew the thirst
   which comes with dying.

When others give of themselves
They point me
To You.

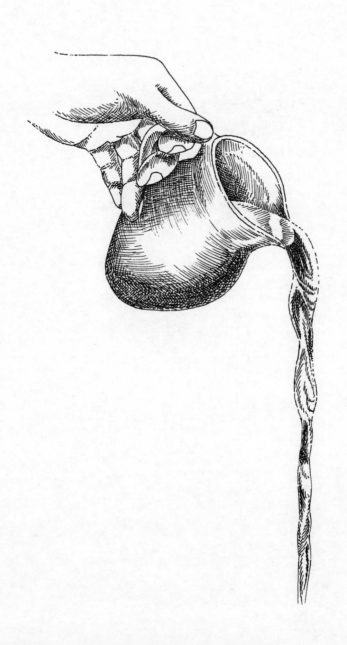

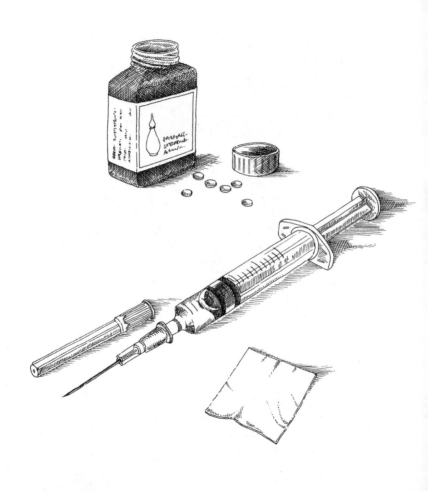

"You've drugs for the pain
and drugs for the nausea
Just shout if you need more . . ."

More?
More than that needle and syringe
with tiny impregnated antiseptic
to wipe away the trace where it went in?
More than little white pills
proffered on clean hands?
They are my treatment.

". . . All right?"

"All right."

A smile exchanged
but not with my eyes.
A wave goodbye
A car driving away

There is no more

And a tear falls quietly
quickly rubbed away

Lord, guard me from self-pity.
You, too, were not comforted.
Your friends slept,
unaware of Your inward struggles

Engender in me
a sensitivity towards others
which I long for them to show towards me

Engender in me
a sensitivity towards You:
because I only ever glimpse Your struggles.

Do You clam up
   when Your words are trampled on;
   when You share what is precious
   and find it mocked;
Do You want to take back Your gesture?

     Do You wish you had not spoken
       when You are not understood
       when Your meaning is
       misinterpreted
        misquoted
        distorted
     Until it is sapped of Your love?

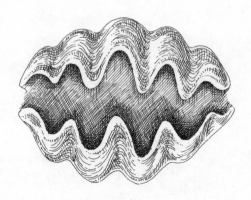

When You try to show love
   with its hurt
   and its pain
   but ears are deaf
   and eyes are blind
   by hands which cover them –
Does Your trying want to give up?

And yet You persist
You forgive, You forbear
With Your promise:
You're God, and not man

               Lord, make me like You!
               That my love may be more
               Forgiving

                          like Yours.

"How are you?"

The question is asked;
I'll put out feelers
Tentatively.
If they care, they'll release me to say more

"It's not been a good week."
    "Oh dear; glad you're better now though dear.
    Glad to see you – I wanted to talk . . ."
Better?
Who said that I feel better?
Because I've dragged myself out,
put on a dress
and smiled?
    Say no more, Jane.
    Just listen.

"How are you?"
"I've been a bit sore actually."
    "Poor you. Yes, I've had a sore foot, too.
    Broke it years ago. I'll tell you about it . . ."
Draw alongside.
Say no more, Jane.
Just listen.

Is this what You do, Lord?
Just listen?
No chance to speak
For our moaning
    and droning
about ourselves, our trivia.
Repetitively.

Teach me to pray:
    to stop informing You
    of history You already know.

When I ask You to speak,
   may Your word not simply remind me of myself.
   May I listen wholly
   And feel with You
   And think with You
   And picture You
      in all I hear You say.

They all stand round my iron bed
This entourage of learners
All seeking to learn
Seeking to help
All in awe
Of the big white chief

Yet none draws near
Nor holds my arm
They're discussing my case
As if it were history
Not living

And questions are asked
They stammer replies
To prove knowledge, show skill,
Earn points for promotion
Inflating their status
For the big white chief

"Any more questions?"
  – Yes, I had some!
But faces now turn
All enquiring, none sharing,
  – Perhaps I have none
    After all . . .

    You are Almighty
    Yet Your drawing near
    Does not make me feel small;
    For You come right down
    As servant, though King,
    Not whipping up fear
    But deepening kinship
    So we become one.

When pain was great
I gave
whispering,
"For You, Lord, I'll do it!"

They did not know
the cost to me

They saw no pain
so they could not recognize
the sacrifice

And they accused,
"You did not give enough!"

> So now I want
> to resent
> to be angry
> to shout, like a child,
> "They're not fair!"

> I want
> to laugh at Your command
> that we should give
> and never count the cost

Yet, You give
when we do not know
nor appreciate
the cost to You

You give
when we do not see
nor recognize
Your sacrifice

You give
though Your pain is great
whispering,
"For you, whom I love, I'll do it!"

It shouts so loudly!
  that smile, so plastic
  the gaze, so unfeeling
  the handshake, so held at arm's length . . .
    Does she really ask after me in love?

I need an enquiry to seem more genuine
To see lips move with loving comfort,
Not part enough only to let words be forced out
  As if sharing the minimum in hurt
  As if mouthing an emptiness of sound

I want to feel hands reaching out
Imparting courage with gentle hold:
Not pulling back after routine gesture
  as if to hug their own lap
  as if that's where care really lies . . .

    Yet, she has come to me
    She has enquired how I am.
    Oh, my Lord,
    Help me not to withdraw from her!

For You never withdraw from me.
  When I come to You
  You do not send me away
    until I am more genuine.

When I try to speak to You,
You do not stand back and say,
  "See her lips move with words she doesn't understand!"

    You accept whatever I offer to You
    You accept me as I am.
    And so I dare to come to You
    More genuinely each time.

How can I say how I feel;
How portray a true picture;
How convey the aloneness of pain
    When others don't give time to listen?

        Oh! I get by
        (I may feel that I can't)
        Life's machine carries on
        Somehow . . .

And you, my God?
  A Bridegroom
  Whose bride will not give
  an embrace
  for her flirting with others

  A Father
  Whose child will not meet
  tender gaze
  for his busyness looking elsewhere

Your pain is of loving
  an unrequited love;
Your aloneness is enduring
  backs turned on You;

How can You say how You feel about that;
How do You paint a true picture?
How convey Your constant forgiveness
    When we don't give time to listen?

I saw a most beautiful plant today;
probably, no-one has noticed it before.
Rich depth of colour hung from the stem.
What a privilege for me to see it,
high upon that lonely hill!

    Why did You make it, Lord?
    Why do You sustain its life?

My eyes turned pensively away
and suddenly I realized that there was
a whole sea of these plants.
Yet none of them radiated colour
as the first.

That one was exquisite;
that one plant stood out on all the hillside
    because the light of the sun shone behind and through it.

Could it be that that plant was me?
An ordinary being among a sea of others . . .
unnoticeable, except when I am seen
    with the Light of the Son shining behind and through me?

And could it be that that one plant
was a parable on my suffering?
For all that I see is my suffering . . .
But could it be that others see
the rich depth of colour hanging from that stem?
    Beauty suspended
    dependent on
    the suffering?

If that is so, then no longer can I ask,
    Why did You make me, Lord?
    Why do You sustain my life?

For I'm grateful that I could feast my eyes upon those
    colours.
So if that's what You do in my life,
    then what a privilege for me to live it!

A bird with clipped wings
cannot fly

But you shall fly
dearest child of God;
you shall fly

Yet you shall be different
bitter sweet
blessing and burden

In your aloneness together
may your family be
close together

In their reaching (though groping)
may you not doubt their motives:
always loving

And in their nurturing
may their protection
not be a bitter boundary

Fly, Elizabeth Joy, fly!
little bird with clipped wings

Paula died on Saturday
And we are left, alive

    It was so easy:
    just one step
    the end of one breath
    and then, all effort was ended

It could have been me
Who had made that one step!
You gave me a taste
Then asked me to stay . . .

    But Paula You called
    to such fullness of Life
    that our prison of grief
    feels a second-best place

Paula died on Saturday
And we are left . . . alive?

    No!
    We are half dead:
    Lord God
    be our Life!

    Even here, as we are
    draw closer, yet closer
    until You are
    our very breath

Part VI

FESTIVITY
Celebrations through the year

Arise, shine, for your light has come,
and the glory of the Lord rises upon you.
Isaiah 60:1

This I call to mind
and therefore I have hope:
Because of the Lord's great love
we are not consumed . . .
Lamentations 3:21–22

I listened recently to a concert of music by Tchaikovsky. His fifth symphony apparently represents his attempts to defeat his homosexuality: attempts which were in vain. And so the symphony ends with the same haunting theme as it began.

The programme note asked rhetorically, "Has not the voyage of hope been merely in a circle from which there is no escape?"

At times my own life seems to be just that. Hopes for release from pain are repeatedly dashed. For all of us at times, life seems like an endless round, in which one is travelling in circles. Anniversaries can become like a measure of the lack of progress; a reminder that circumstances have not changed. And annual festivities can be so routine that they become memorials to repetition and stagnation.

Yet, as a fire is never still, though it is constant, so too are we ever changing, ever being remoulded. For, as long as the fire of our life remains alight, there is constant movement: the movement of flames dancing, of flickering embers being rekindled, of flashes of inspiration, or the more painful times when life itself seems more like a furnace. And so there is always a place for celebration.

This section was written at significant festivals during the year while I was compiling this book, capturing with my pen those places where I stumbled upon fresh aspects of God. For He does not repeat the same blessings year after year, merely topping us up as if with routine gifts. He reveals new and different aspects of Himself and His truth.

While hope for rescue from our circumstances might die, as did Tchaikovsky's, our hope in God can never be consumed.

52

(Christmas)

You've been born in my life
You're welcome
And I've decorated the place
For You to come in
And with tinsel, and lights, and music
I celebrate Your birth in me

But You came
not to the place which is light
but into the dark places
into a hidden stable
at the back

And You ask
to be born today
in my dark places
my hidden areas
in the recesses of my being
among the dung of my life
where no preparation is made

You want it lit
not by my festive candles
but by the single flame
of Your life beginning
even in that stench

And I'm told of Your glory
by angels announcing
that You have crept in
And now I dare to look
into the backyard of my heart
And I worship You

53

(New Year)

The greeting is passed around the church,
"Happy New Year!"
And I watch,
cynicism rising.

What do those smiling words mean?
How can they ring true?
Are we hoping for events to change,
    for Sheila's cancer to vanish
    for Roger's working hours to diminish
    for Heather's young mourning to end?
And are others wishing
for my pain to cease
with one simple greeting?
    Empty optimism!

Lord God, save us from disillusionment.
Save us from wrong hope.

May we long
not for the smoothness of sand
which looks good, and feels flat,
and is easy to walk on
but will not withstand a storm

May we build our hopes
on You.
Though You may not prevent the storms
You keep us firm
within them

So even if we're battered
we cannot fall
except deeper into a crevice
in the rock;
deeper into You

54

(Lent)

Can I follow You, this Lent?

Oh, I give of my bounty:
When I've lots, I give You some

But in Your poverty
You gave

After You'd spent
All that You had
All that You were
   Exhausted
No supportive friends
Only barren wilderness

Then, You did not give up
But chose to give
Surrendering to Your Father

You did not give up
Either hope, or trust;
But, remembering promises,
You clung to the truth

Help me, this Lent,
Not to give up
But rather, to give

Not to wait until
Exhaustion is past

But to give of myself
More of myself
   Like You

So, it's today.
Publication of the new book
. . . my book

> And the evenings of slog:
> long hours at my desk
> ("No, I'm sorry.
> I can't come out tonight;
> can't phone for a chat:
> I'm working . . ."
>   "I see."
> They don't see:
> they phone me to chat
> they call to be friendly
> and I'm so pleased . . .
> but my writing is left
> pending)
> . . . my book

And the mornings of inspiration
while the house was still hushed
when I leaned from my bed
to scribble frenzied words,
pages
(It came quickly, then!)
. . . my book

> And the letters I've posted
> and waited to hear
> did they like it –
> . . . my book?

And the prayer every session
like a trip-wire to catch me
lest I try and write
before turning to You
to tune in to You
because –
> did I nearly forget?
> . . . it's Your book

You are the One
who deserves congratulation:
    so these cards all around me
    I'll offer to You;
    and these balloons brought for fun
    I'll hang up for You;
    and this single red rose
    (it's a sign of deep love) –
        will You take that as well?
        I'd like it that way
        . . . to thank You

Seldom do I give You a card
or balloons
or flowers;
but in celebrating today
I'm brought to remember –
. . . my work, my whole life
is thanks
to You

(Mothering Sunday)

To my son –
and to my Heavenly Father

The times I most treasure
were those feeds in the night
I used to creep through
at first sound of your cry

And you lay in my arms
and you gazed as you looked
and I rocked in the chair
and I sang
and you cooed

We'd have melted the frosts
by the warmth in our hearts
When the world was asleep
and they danced in their dreams
we danced in our eyes

And that is the closeness
You long for, my Father
Yet I'm blind to Your tenderness
and shrink from Your hold
Rouse me from slumber
to lie in Your arms
and gaze in sheer wonder
at the warmth in Your eyes.

(On our wedding anniversary)

I'm here, my love,
I'm still here

I'll stay near to you, my love,
Close at your side
In all your work I'll encourage you
For I'm here, my love,
I'm still here

I'll listen to your tales, my love
I'll enquire of your days
And I'll smile with warm pleasure
With you
For I'm here, my love,
I'm still here

We'll walk hand in hand again, my love,
For long hours we shall sit
Watching waves, together
For I'm here, my love,
I'm still here

Farewells were not far away, my love,
Yet, not harsh
They were softened by knowing
We'd have met again, one day,
We'd have met again

But rejoice, my love!
For I'm here
I'm still here,
My love.

(Good Friday)

The procession was long
and silent.
One man alone
carried the cross
    struggling beneath its wearisome weight
    stumbling over the rough road's ridges:
He helped us to focus on Christ.

The procession trailed
in silence.
Even children were quiet
Shrill voices hushed
Eyes fixed on the cross which,
    alone,
spoke
like Your still small voice

Up the noisy high street –
    and loudest of all
    was the Hi-Fi shop
    blaring out the Top Ten hits:
    trashy, tinny sound! –
in silence
a procession of witness
reminding the world
(reminding ourselves!)
of the day You died

They did not hear
that still, small voice.
They did not hear the Good News
for listening to
whatever whim was best that week

Some stopped to watch
and nodded a smile
"Oh yes: Good Friday today."
But Bank Holidays are busy days
and they were very busy

So, looking back to shopping chores
sweet smiles turned sour
in their repose
embittered at the God
who no longer speaks, they say.

Forgive us, Father
Your voice is so small, so still
and this world clamours so loudly
— we don't know what we say.

59

(Easter)

Once it happened
in Holy Week
Oh, how I trembled
at the timing!

For, from elation
at being clapped
by hundreds of people

I first slid
then plummeted
as into an airless mine
suffocating
    in pain

That filled my heart
with fear:
Fear that, so soon,
I can cascade to death.
So soon . . .

Then I trembled again
at the timing:

Do You ask
each one to identify
with Your sufferings?

Is this — somehow —
completing Your sufferings?

I want to shrink back
from pain
Yet I am torn:
for my heart longs
to embrace whatever You ask . . .

And then, Easter Day.
Suddenly, unsummoned,
the realization

That my heavy stone
had been rolled to one side

Revealing this grave of darkness
as nothing but an empty cavern

Yawning in its open-ness
to be filled afresh
with praise

Lord, how I tremble
at Your timing.

60

(Ascension Day)

The song of the skylark
ascending from silent moors
stills my soul

And in its wake, I anticipate
the sweet music of Your voice
which penetrates my silence
when I wait before You

Raise my spirit to Your heights
until I'm flying next to You
ascending still
until I'm out of sight

Still heard
singing a soft duet
with You

Appendix

1   As inevitably . . .   We are all on a journey to God. Ecclesiastes 1:7: "All streams flow into the sea."
  Even where I only touch Him with one part of me, then I am "filled with all the fulness of God" (Ephesians 3:19 RSV). This is the place where my self-centred ego is lost, and replaced by the flavour of salt; the flavour of God.

2   There's a score across the sky . . .   Jesus frequently touched people in order to heal them, or give them strength, or simply to impart courage. It is the touch of His Spirit which continually gives perspective to all the scars, physical and mental, which I carry.
  Mark 8:22: "They begged Jesus to touch him."

3   With hypnotic rhythm . . .   Written on the shores at Arisaig; in the same little inlet as the significant Chapter 2 of A Harvest from Pain (1989) which became the basis of that book. This was where Philippa found her bread-shaped stone.

4   The spider, falling . . .   However precariously we may be dangling from a thread, Jesus' promise that He holds us means we will be kept completely safe. John 10:28: "No-one can snatch them out of my Father's hand."

5   Your goodness sometimes seems . . .   Whenever God's goodness seems elusive, I return to a verse which came alive to me during 1980 (as described in Chapter 8 of A Pathway Through Pain (1987)). Lamentations 3:22 RSV: "The steadfast love of the Lord never ceases; His mercies never come to an end."

6   How I long to be bubbly again . . .   As Jesus poured Himself out on the cross, He quoted Psalm 31:5: "Into your hands I commit my spirit."

7   It's dark . . .   Those who know illness know that to leave the curtains open at night-time strangely offers company. Even one doctor friend, Jenny, leaving my bedside one dusk, suggested, "Shall I leave your curtains open for company?" The ending of this poem refers to 1 Corinthians 13:12: "Now we see but a poor reflection as in a mirror; then we shall see face to face."

8   Like a mist upon the sea . . .   Another poem from Arisaig (see note 3). John 1:16: "From   the   fulness   of   his   grace

we have all received one blessing after another." But it is all undeserved, Ephesians 1:9, "according to God's good pleasure".

9   I hear the voice of sleep . . .   This was written in 1971 during months of an obscure and most debilitating encephalitis-type virus. I was sixteen.

10   Wind-blown, leaf-swept . . .   Written in November 1986 when illness seemed to take a very solemn turn. It was robbing me of many aspects of life, and by contrast I wanted to cling to every ability I had left, for as long as possible.

   Mark 8:35: "Whoever wants to save his life will lose it, but whoever loses his life for me and for the gospel will save it."

PART II   FLAMES

11   My eyes like to see . . .   My son Angus wrote this poem in school. I include it here because I feel his young spirituality, coupled with his firm hope in God, is an inspiration. It is like a flame, ignited perhaps by the sparks which fly off my own faith and Matthew's. His theme of shining reflects Philippians 2:15, "You shine like stars in the universe as you hold out the word of life".

12   Hungrily . . .   This is one of many pieces written in Fazakerley hospital while I was profoundly ill during May/June 1989.

   My initial intense frustration at being withdrawn from active life, yet again, eventually gave way to a new contentment in my relationship with God. I was freshly dependent on stillness and being, rather than activity in prayer.

   Psalm 46:10: "Be still and know that I am God."

13   Let me dare . . .   (See note 12). The phrase from the Lord's Prayer, "Your will be done" took on a new significance in my hospital bed when my ability to "do" God's will had to become a more submissive allowing of His will to be done in me.

14   At times when it's calm . . .   Another poem from Arisaig (see note 3).

   Hebrews 8:9: "I took them by the hand to lead them."

15   I pray for Your strength . . .   When prayer seems not to be answered, I bow before Him all the more because I realize that He is God, not I. My ways, with my pain-free, easy solutions, are not His ways (Isaiah 55:8).

   Lamentations 3:32–33: "Though he brings grief, he will show compassion, so great is his unfailing love. For he does not willingly bring affliction or grief to the children of men."

16 Too often . . . Written while life seemed to revolve around taking doses of medicine, when I saw how we can insult our Father by treating prayer as a medicine.

Isaiah 58:11: "You will be like a well-watered garden, like a spring whose waters never fail."

17 Switch off the television . . . Written for my husband Matthew, during the Ethiopian famine in 1985. Our concern for others, however insignificant or even impotent it may seem, shines as a light which dispels despair.

Matthew 5:13,14: "You are the salt of the earth . . . You are the light of the world."

18 Sorry your wife has walked out . . . I believe that God shares our sufferings and feels our pain with us at a depth we can never fully grasp.

Isaiah 63:9: "In all their distress, he too was distressed."

19 You hear the cries of many . . . This was written while I was praying for one person in particular in September 1986, though I suspect that it could be for anyone engaged in full-time ministry.

Matthew 11:28: "Come to me, all you who are weary and burdened, and I will give you rest."

20 Blue flowers . . . I believe that Jesus' deepest healing for us is to open us towards Him.

Mark 7:34: "With a deep sigh (Jesus) said to him, 'Ephphatha!' (which means, 'Be opened!')"

PART III   FURNACE

21 It's like an Arctic hibernation . . . While setting feelings into words about the alone-ness of pain, I realized that this isolation is similar to what the mystics call a "desert experience". It is an experience in which God, though He seems distant, makes Himself known most unexpectedly. Hence the poem can end with great hope.

Exodus 3:2 GNB: "The angel of the Lord appeared to (Moses) as a flame coming from the middle of a bush."

22 They say . . . This short piece was written while I was heavily drugged in Fazakerley hospital, May/June 1989 (see note 12).

1 Peter 4:13 GNB: "Rather, be glad that you are sharing Christ's sufferings, so that you may be full of joy when his glory is revealed."

23 The corridor of my life . . . Luke 1:78–79: "The rising sun will come to us from heaven to shine on those living in darkness and in the shadow of death, to guide our feet into the path of peace."

24 Pain's constrictions . . . I pictured, as I wrote, those old-fashioned types of corset whose strings had to be pulled tighter and tighter in order to make its wearer look more glamorous. The ensuing restriction looks quite suffocating! And so, similarly, is pain, pulling tighter and tighter. But Stephen's drawing shows that, beneath the broken chain (myself) is the unbreakable supporting strength which represents Jesus' solid hold. God's freedom is not restricted to being out of prison, or out of pain, or out of corsets! His freedom is also found within the restrictions.

Romans 8:23 GNB: "We wait for God to make us his sons and set our whole being free."

25 It is the easy way . . . Written in Fazakerley hospital (see note 12). To think about what pain prevents me from doing is very easy, but wrong. It is a sign that I am not trusting God to have my life under His control.

Matthew 7:14 GNB: "The gate to life is narrow and the way that leads to it is hard, and there are few people who find it."

26 Screens drawn securely round . . . Stephen's picture, with its screens so close to the bed, shows clearly how insular any patient can become while cut off from others. This is compounded when visitors come with the aim of helping the patient, yet deny that patient the privilege of giving.

St Francis of Assisi said, "It is in giving that we receive . . ."

27 Tonight . . . Pain is only destructive when we fail to take God's hand in it; but then it is amazingly transformed into a vehicle for growth.

2 Corinthians 12:9: "My power is made perfect in weakness."

28 Do not kiss me now . . . One of my favourite poems. Even the most mundane things, when offered to God, can be transformed out of all worldly recognition.

29 My life is on fire . . . Neither the burning bush seen by Moses (Exodus 3) nor the furnace where Shadrach, Meshach and Abednego were thrown, consumed.

Isaiah 43:2: "When you walk through the fire, you will not be burned; the flames will not set you ablaze."

30 Do not weep . . . A heartfelt prayer dedicated to Matthew (see also poem 57). The resurrection hope is very strong, and was at the forefront of my mind when I wrote this in Fazakerley hospital, May/June 1989 (see note 12).

But heaven is not the only place of miracles. Christ's first miracle was to change water into wine. John 2:9: "and the master of the banquet tasted the water that had been turned into wine". I believe

Jesus can also change our watery tears into something very special and acceptable to Him.

Stephen's drawing hints at this transformation. Around the weeping figure's raised arm, he has shaded the shape which is a chalice.

31 I've been dreaming . . . Written in Fazakerley hospital (see note 12). It was hard to trust that God's purpose could be fulfilled through such severe sickness. I was consoled by Isaiah 55:8,9: "My ways are not your ways." Only a vision of Christ Himself can ever extinguish the tendency to self-pity which is known so well to anyone in pain.

PART IV FLICKERS

32 If I lift my eyes . . . God is not only to be found in the heights of achievement.

Psalm 139:8: "If I go up to the heavens, you are there; if I make my bed in the depths, you are there."

33 Limp curtain . . . At Pentecost the coming of the Holy Spirit sounded like a wind, Acts 2:2: "Suddenly a sound like the blowing of a violent wind came from heaven and filled the whole house where they were sitting."

34 When I cling to what I want . . . Ivy clings on to a tree, stifling growth and causing the effect of choking. And if you tie a young tree wrongly, then instead of the tie expanding with the tree's growth, it actually strangles the tree.

So within my own life. If I do not allow God to remove the "ivy" then my spiritual growth will be choked. John 12:24–25: "Unless a grain of wheat falls to the ground and dies, it remains only a single seed . . . The man who loves his life will lose it, while the man who hates his life in this world will keep it for eternal life."

35 Yesteryear's streams . . . Stephen's drawing is from a photograph taken in Spain at the height of a hot summer drought. The unexpected colour of the bushes in the middle of the river-bed was very striking, standing out as they did from the dry valley. They were the only sign that a stream had once flowed there – but sign they were.

Psalm 1:3 and Jeremiah 17:7–8: "The man who trusts in the Lord . . . is like a tree planted by the water, that sends out its roots by the stream."

36 At rock bottom . . . Matthew 5:14,16: "You are the light of the world . . . let your light shine before men, that they may . . . praise your Father in heaven." (See also note 49.)

37   My heaviness reminds me . . .   Convalescence is a wearisome time and the idea of reading the Bible or of praying is far from its usual joy and inspiration. Indeed it can be one of the most dreaded ideas! It was this heaviness which prompted my thinking.

38   When those things I cannot do . . .   Whether my "enemies" are other people who seem not to understand, or whether they are tauntings within me, God's promises still hold true: such as Jeremiah 1:19, "They will fight against you but will not overcome you, for I am with you, and will rescue you."

39   Do I dare ask for Your kind of care? . . .   Sometimes my awareness that I fall so far short of Christ's example causes me almost to despair of even trying. But even the smallest gesture towards goodness, made in His name, is like offering a tiny seed which God promises He'll cause to grow.
   Matthew 13:32: "The mustard seed . . . though it is the smallest of all your seeds, yet when it grows, it is the largest of garden plants."

40   Caught off guard . . .   I am grateful to Stephen for the inspiration in his interpretation of this poem. The tumbling waterfall emphasizes that yielding to temptation is like falling. Lively splashes at the foot of the drop show the pleasant, dancing lure of impure thoughts "which entice me"; the swirling undercurrents (highlit in the small repeat) warn of the nature of temptation which sucks us into an unexpectedly strong downward pull.

PART V   FLARES

41   That nurse over there . . .   That nurse was like a fore-runner of Christ, allowing the flame of God's light to be seen in her in the same way as a runner carries the Olympic torch.
   Philippians 2:5–7: "Your attitude should be the same as that of Christ Jesus, who, being in very nature God, did not consider equality with God something to be grasped, but made himself nothing, taking the very nature of a servant . . ."

42   You've drugs for the pain . . .   At the time of Jesus' worst struggle, in Gethsemane, no other human being knew nor shared in what He was going through. How often I am saved from self-pity by reminding myself of that fact!
   Mark 14:37: "Are you asleep? Could you not keep watch for one hour?"

43   Do you clam up? . . .   (See also note 48). God's nature is in stark contrast to mine. He never closes. I believe He is a vulnerable God: He allows His words to be trampled on, mocked, misinterpreted, misquoted. Yet He always remains open.

Hosea 11:7–9: "My people are determined to turn from me . . . (But) how can I give you up, Ephraim? How can I hand you over, Israel? . . . For I am God, and not man – the Holy One among you. I will not come in wrath."

44 How are you? . . . So often we can do things – even pray – with the intention of making ourselves feel good for doing it.

Philippians 2:3: "Do nothing out of selfish ambition or vain conceit, but in humility consider others better than yourselves."

45 They all stand round . . . Not only have I lain in a hospital bed myself, surrounded by the many doctors on the Grand Round, but also as a nursing sister I have watched my patients be awed into suppressing all their questions. The arrival of "The Chief" in the ward engenders a hushed respect which silences any relaxed dialogue. It is in marked contrast to Jesus' coming alongside us.

Philippians 2:6–7: "Who, being in very nature God, did not consider equality with God something to be grasped, but made himself nothing, taking the very nature of a servant . . ."

46 When pain was great . . . How often do I fail to see what Christ has suffered, in order to give to me? Yet He does not give in order to be thanked. Even while He was being mocked, spat upon, sneered, He lovingly gave forgiveness and astonishing freedom.

Luke 23:34: "Father, forgive them, for they do not know what they are doing."

47 It shouts so loudly! . . . One friend urged me to omit this poem because it reveals the worst side of me. Unfortunately, though, a part of me is not kind. This was not written to impress others; it was written to God.

The only way I could cope with the apparent hardness of the plastic smile was to tell my Father about it. In doing so, I found comfort and also challenge.

I do not believe that God expects us to be so polite towards Him that we avoid talking with Him about how things are! And if we're honest, I suspect we can all admit to being unkind sometimes. Through bringing that to Him, we glimpse, by contrast, the outstanding forgiveness of God.

48 How can I say how I feel . . . The whole book of Hosea speaks of God's faithfulness to us even when we are faithless to Him. It is to this that I turn when I feel let down by others' apparent lack of care; for my let-down and disappointment is nothing in comparison to what God endures constantly from us. To emulate His light, we are to keep showing love.

Hosea 3:1: "The Lord said to me, 'Go, show your love to your wife again, though she is loved by another and is an adulteress.'"

49   I saw a most beautiful plant today . . .   I wrote this on the slopes of Ben Vorlich in April 1981. Still lacking strength after the traumas and major operations the previous year, I was unable to reach the top and instead I lay in the grass while Matthew walked on alone.

My mind was heavy about two things. First, Elizabeth Joy had just been born with Down's syndrome (see note 50). But there was also my own life. *A Pathway Through Pain* (1987) tells how hard it was to come to terms with not dying, after coming so close to such release in 1980.

The discovery of this flower was my turning point, the moment of acceptance of life with its severe limitations. Now harebells (illustrated) are a most apt token, frequently presented to me by a friend, Sandy, to remind me that God's light shines through me no matter how limited I feel. And the same is true for Elizabeth Joy.

50   A bird with clipped wings . . .   Elizabeth Joy was born with Down's syndrome. She is the firstborn of friends of ours, both graduates, who had hoped for a normal, intelligent child. I found myself sharing very deeply in the sadness at her handicap, and this poem was one of many pieces I wrote when she was born in April 1981. See also poem 49, written thinking of Elizabeth Joy as well as of myself.

51   Paula died on Saturday . . .   Paula's death in March 1989 hit me very hard. We had been very similar, both in personality and in the disease which struck us both. And then suddenly she died, and I was left.

In thinking of her death, I became fascinated by the creativity of the breath of God.

Genesis 2:7 GNB: "(God) breathed life-giving breath into his nostrils and the man began to live."

Ezekiel 37:6 GNB: "I will put breath into you and bring you back to life."

John 20:22: "Jesus breathed on them and said, 'Receive the Holy Spirit.'"

PART VI   FESTIVITY

52   (Christmas)   You've been born in my life . . .   God's choice of a dirty stable for the arrival of His Son to be with us is in sharp contrast to the glittery stuff we drape around. I wonder if our commercial festivities actually re-create the "No room" signs which He found in Bethlehem.

Luke 2:7: "She placed him in a manger, because there was no room for them in the inn."

53 (New Year) The greeting is passed . . . Words of greeting in Beverley Minster (January 1989) sounded very empty when, only the previous evening, I had heard friends talk of their deep suffering. Then a little child wriggled on to my knee, thrusting the story of the wise and foolish men (Matt. 7:24) for me to read to her. Suddenly the whispered story pointed to the fact that trusting in God does not protect us from storms. Even the wise man had to face a storm; but he was protected within it. With that simple story I could find a realistic hope for my friends.

54 (Lent) Can I follow You this Lent? . . . There is a compelling difference between giving up, giving in, and giving. Lent is considered a time to give something up. It was a time when Jesus gave. He gave of Himself by being in the wilderness rather than in plenty. See also John 10:17 GNB: "I am willing to give up my life . . ."

55 (Publication day) So, it's today . . . Of all five books, the writing of *A Pathway Through Pain* was a particular response to God's prompting. Rarely did I attempt to write before praying; when I did, my fingers literally stuck between the typewriter keys or I had pages of crossings-out. I could only liken it to my standing beneath a fountain with a bucket to catch the flow.
  Colossians 3:23: "Whatever you do, work . . . as for the Lord."

56 (Mothering Sunday) The times I most treasure . . . The rapport expressed in the inimitable gaze between parent and child is but a glimpse of the rapport we can reach towards with our Lord.
  Psalm 27:8: "Your face, Lord, I will seek."

57 (Wedding anniversary) I'm here, my love . . . This is dedicated to Matthew, as is poem 30. It was written when I came home from Fazakerley hospital (see note 3).
  Our parting will be but for a short time. 1 Thessalonians 4:17: "And so we will be with the Lord for ever."

58 (Good Friday) The procession was long . . . Written at Heswall, 1989. Elijah heard God's voice not in the earthquake or the fire, but in silence as a still small voice.
  1 Kings 19:12: "After the fire came a gentle whisper."

59 (Easter) Once it happened . . . This was April 1988. I would not presume to say that God *caused* me to suffer that week; but the timing struck such a deep chord that I could identify afresh with His sufferings.
  Philippians 3:10: "I want to know Christ and the power of his resurrection and the fellowship of sharing in his sufferings . . ." (see also Colossians 1:24).

60 (Ascension Day) The song of the skylark . . . In childhood

days we used to hear the skylarks at Gleneagles station in Scotland. We strained to keep sight of the tiny dot in the blue sky, until it was so high we could see it no more. Its echoing song was the first sound of the Highlands. It represented heaven. This is the final poem among those from Fazakerley hospital (see note 12), written at 3 a.m. during one night in June, 1989. My looking towards my own ascension is perhaps an indication of the severity of that spell of illness. It was a source of hope, that I could look forward to being "out of sight" from this world. Death will be an ascension, a climax, to life's aim which is union with God.

And it is a privilege that an author's voice may still be heard even after we are out of sight from this world.

Also published by Hodder & Stoughton:

OPEN TO GOD

Joyce Huggett

Joyce Huggett offers practical guidance on how to use the body and imagination to prepare for prayer and find stillness. The theme of new beginnings makes it ideal for use at the beginning of the year, or whenever the reader is called to a deeper and richer prayer life.

'The great value of this book is that classic spirituality is brought out of the medieval monastery into the living room of a modern semi. It shows how silence, retreats and imaginative contemplation fit into a busy life that is looking for reality with God.'   Rev David Gillett

'A unique resource for a fresh encounter with God.'
                                                      Christian Herald

TEACH US TO PRAY

Joyce Huggett with
Simeon Wood & John Gerighty

This cassette is a natural companion to *Open to God*. It contains two meditations centred around the Scriptures, accompanied by wind instruments and guitar, bringing the biblical text to life through a sustained meditation.

Joyce Huggett says: 'There are as many ways of praying as there are people of prayer. Pray as you can, not as you can't.'

THE STORM AND OTHER STORIES

Jenny Cooke

Cari, weighed down by the burden of poverty, a drunken father and an unwelcome suitor, has a prophetic dream about a storm which hits her island of Anglesey. When it actually happens, it brings unexpected blessing.

The Storm opens this compelling collection of short stories which speak of transforming faith and enduring hope in the face of pain, disappointment and hardship.

THE GUINNESS LEGEND

Michele Guinness

When the first Arthur Guinness founded a small brewery on the banks of the River Liffey in Dublin, he could not have foreseen the dynasty of brewers and bankers, clergymen and missionaries that would emerge. Drawing on diaries and letters, Michele Guinness interweaves the adventures of Henry Grattan, the Billy Graham of his day, with all the successes and failures of this spirited family.

'A fascinating story.'

The Scotsman

'A thorough, informative but above all captivating account of a truly outstanding family.'   *Sunday Tribune, Dublin*

LIGHT IN MY DARKEST NIGHT

Catherine Marshall

An intimate glimpse into Catherine Marshall's 'dark night of the soul'.

Drawn from journals and taped interviews, *Light in my Darkest Night* traces Catherine's slow climb from a spiritual valley of desolation. Few had known about her struggle. Many will identify with it. Now, through the pages of this poignant and compelling book, an unforgettable message of hope is held out to those in pain.